How you began

CONTENTS

How you began	4
As small as the point of a pin	6
Big head and small arms and legs	8
How did you get food in there?	10
The tail and other odd things	12
The third and fourth months	14
The last few months in the womb	16
On your birth-day	18
How did you get in?	21
How are children made?	21
The sperms swim to the egg	24
When you were conceived	26
In the beginning you were very small	28
When you came into the world	30

KESTREL BOOKS

Penguin Books Limited, Harmondsworth, Middlesex, England

Photographs copyright © 1975 by Lennart Nilsson
Text and editing © 1975 by Jan Cornell and Rune Pettersson
English translation copyright © 1975 by Penguin Books Ltd

Drawings on pp. 22–3 by Per Birger Lundquist
Medical adviser Professor Axel Ingleman-Sundberg
English text adviser Dorothy Dallas
Designed by Per Olov Larsson

All rights reserved. No part of this publication may be reproduced, stored in a retrieval system, or transmitted in any form or by any means, electronic, mechanical, photocopying, recording, or otherwise, without the prior permission of the Copyright owner.

Published in Sweden as *Så blev du till* by Albert Bonniers Förlag AB, Stockholm 1975

First published in Great Britain 1975

Reissued 1982
Reprinted 1982 and 1984

ISBN 0 7226 5116 3

Printed in Hong Kong by
Wilture Enterprises (International) Ltd

HOW YOU BEGAN

A STORY IN PICTURES
BY
LENNART NILSSON

KESTREL BOOKS

How you began

Father, mother and baby immediately after baby was born.

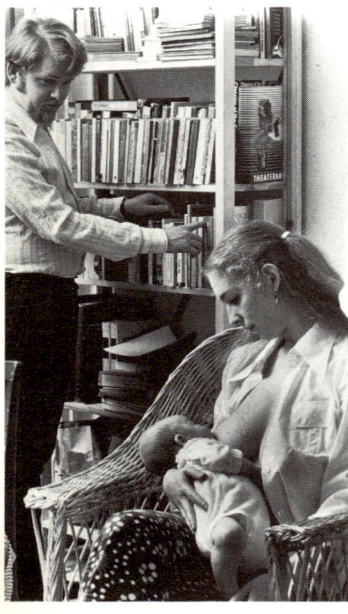

Babies are hungry and like to get milk from mother's breast. In the mother's milk there is everything a baby needs and it can live on this milk and nothing else for **many months**. Babies can also get food out of a bottle or be fed with a spoon.

Everyone was once a child and every child came out of a mother. All children grow; you are growing now, and you will grow for many more years until you are *fully* grown! But even before you were born, you grew inside your mother for nine whole months.

The body of every human is made up of millions of tiny parts called cells. These cells stick together and work together, helping and supporting each other. Cells which have jobs to do work together in groups such as the groups of cells which make up your eyes, your ears, your heart – but where did these cells come from?

Once you were only one cell big, but that cell was a fertilized egg cell, about the size of the point of a pin. (Fertilized eggs grow into animals. The hens' eggs in the shops are not fertilized – otherwise there would be chickens inside them.) From this one cell inside your mother, you grew into two cells, then into four, then more and more, getting bigger all the time, until, finally, you grew into millions of cells. And these cells were all the time getting organized into groups, to make your heart, your stomach, your legs, your arms, which, because they are organized to do special work, are called organs!

Inside your mother it was nice and warm, and you were protected. When you had been growing there for nine months and weighed about seven and a half pounds, you were born and came out of your mother's tummy. Do you know how tall you were and how much you weighed when you were born? All children are weighed and measured just after they are born.

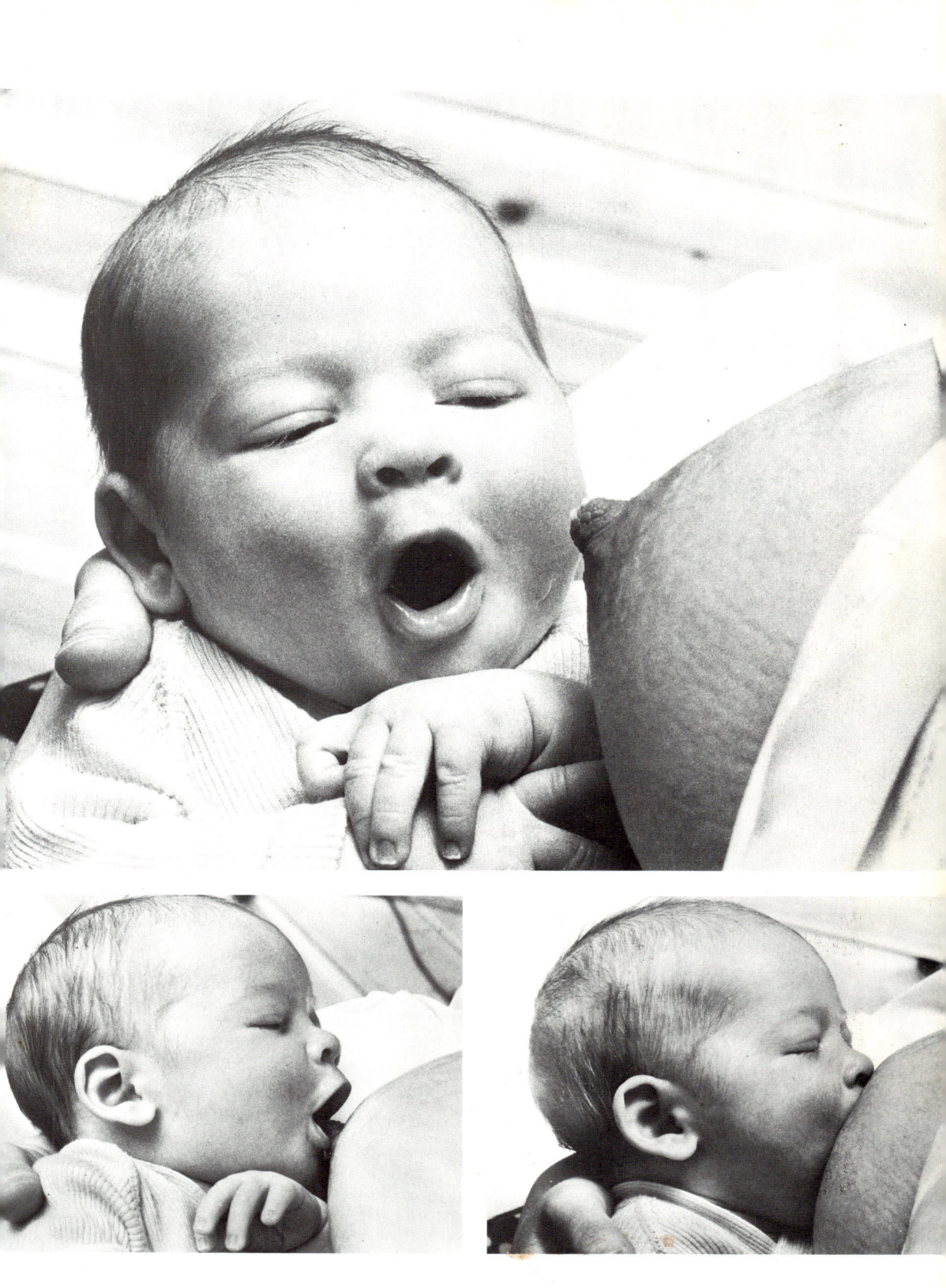

As small as the point of a pin

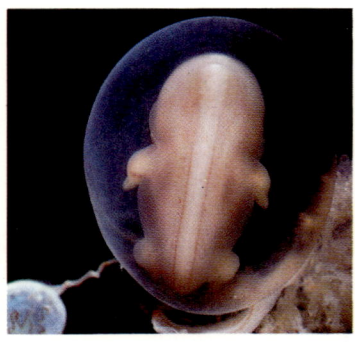

When you had been only four weeks in your mother's womb you looked like a little worm. You can see the head to the left; the round circle is the beginning of something that will become an eye.

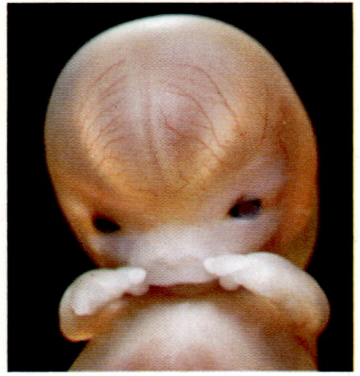

This is the way you looked from behind when you were a six-week-old foetus. On top you see the neck because the head is bent forward. You can also clearly see what are going to be arms and legs.

When you were seven weeks old you had eyes, nose and mouth. But your fingers were not very long yet.

Inside your mother's tummy there is a hollow organ called the womb. And you were inside that, in a 'bubble'. You were lying in a fluid which is very like water. It is called the amniotic fluid. While the baby is there, inside its mother, it is called a foetus and the 'bubble' is called the amnion. In the pictures you can see how the foetus lies in the amnion inside the womb. In the picture on the right the foetus is seven weeks old. It is turned sideways so you can see the head, arms and legs. The picture is made bigger and the foetus is larger than it would really be so that you can see it properly.

Many of the pictures in this book have been made bigger – they have been enlarged. Very small foetuses can only be seen with a microscope which makes things seem a great deal bigger than they are.

When you were lying in there, in the amniotic fluid, you floated around fairly freely. It didn't matter if you were upside down or right side up then. In the little picture at the top on the left you can see how funny you looked before you grew so big that your head and arms and legs could be seen clearly. At first you were as small as the point of a pin. Then you grew into something like a small crooked worm. When four weeks had passed your arms and legs began to show, but you had not grown fingers and toes yet. Already after seven weeks you started looking like a little baby, but your head was very big compared to your body.

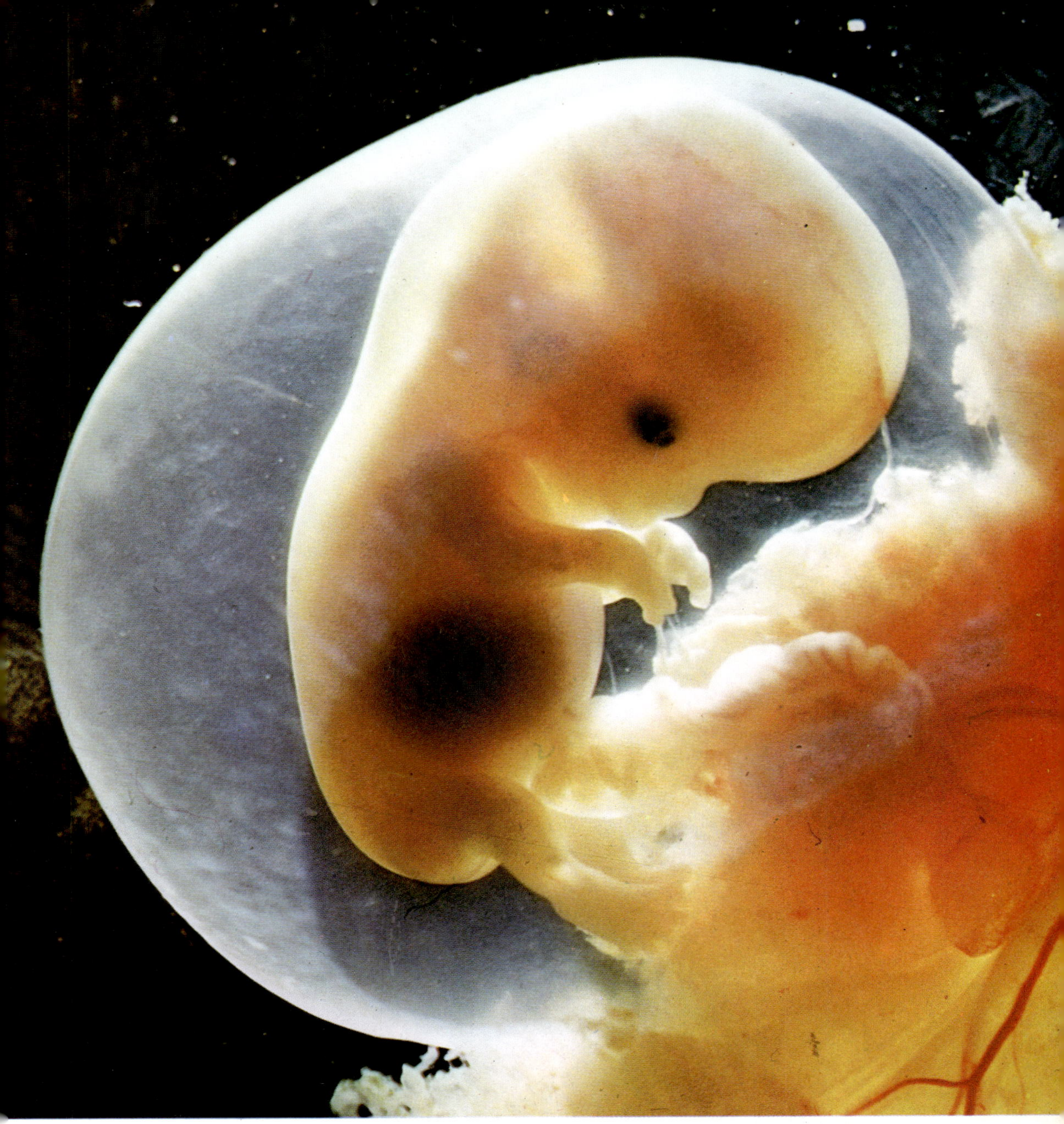

In the enlarged picture above you can see what you looked like when you had been lying in your mother's tummy for seven weeks. In the beginning the head grows faster than other parts. That is why it looks very big here.

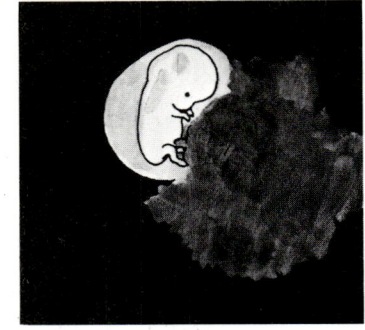

This drawing shows how big you actually were when you were seven weeks old.

Big head and small arms and legs

When you had been inside your mother for about seven weeks you began to look like a baby, but your head was bigger and your legs shorter, much shorter than those of a new-born baby. Different parts of the body grow at different speeds. The head grows most quickly in the beginning. Even when a baby is born you can see that the head is a much bigger part of the whole body than it is in a grown person. The other parts grow more slowly and get finished later.

It was when you were as big as this that your mother became sure that she was going to have a baby. She noticed it in different ways – first, because she did not get her monthly period (called menstruation), the little bleeding she has once a month through the slit between her legs. All girls get that bleeding in the end. Some start when they are only 9 years old, but others not until they are 16.

Small chubby fingers and a pug-nose – that is what all foetuses have after nine weeks inside the mother. They are $1\frac{1}{2}$ inches [4 centimetres] long, the eyes are half-open and the head still bent forward.

A foetus is small and rather transparent so you can see the bones of the skeleton in the hands and feet. You can see the fingernails as well.

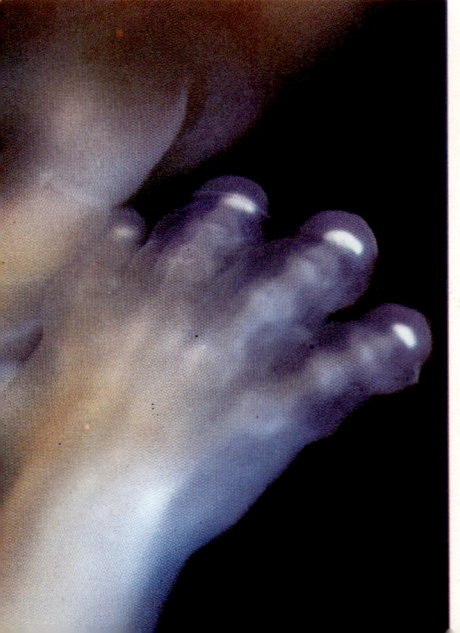
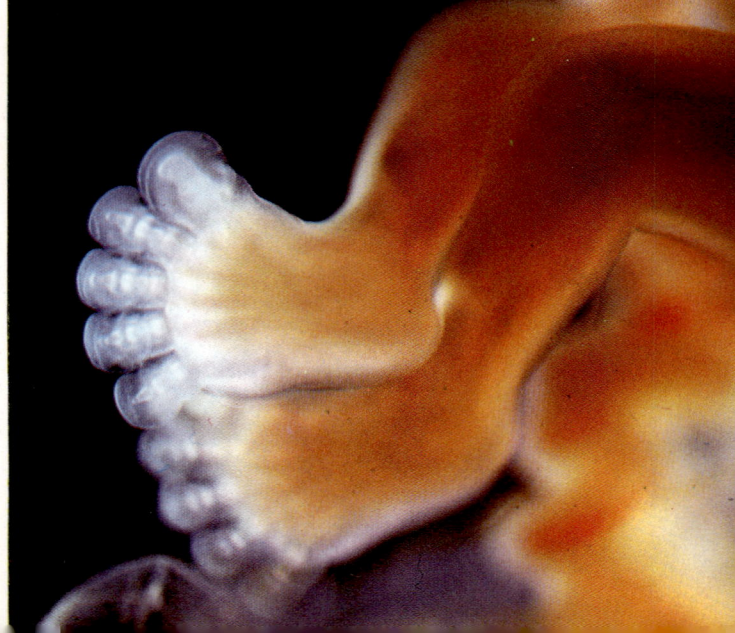

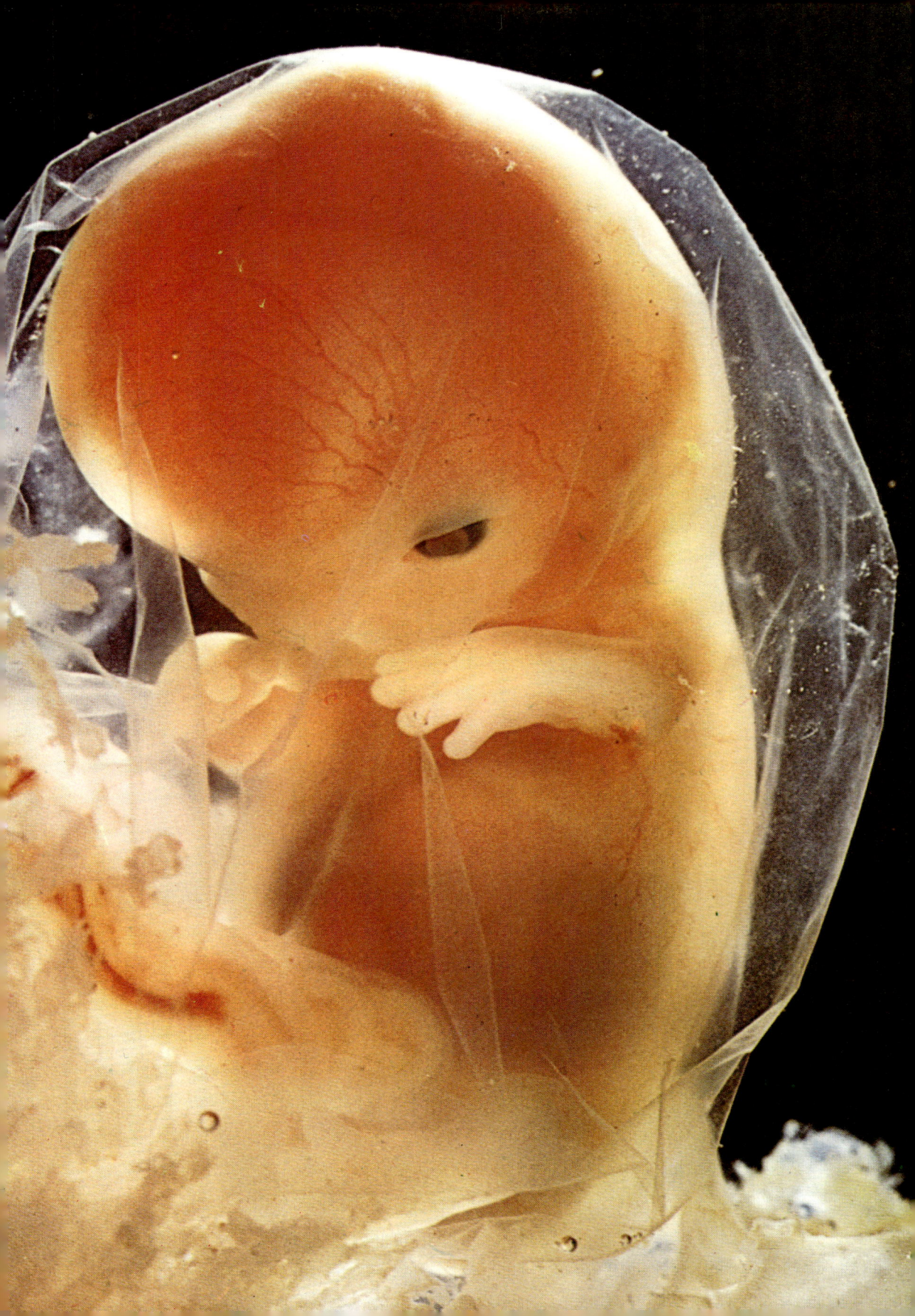

How did you get food in there?

When you eat, you put food into your mouth and after you have chewed and swallowed it, the food gets into your stomach and from there into your intestine. The food has everything you need to keep alive and grow, and this is what is called nourishment. In the intestine the nourishment is taken from the food and transferred into the blood. The blood vessels carry the nourishment around everywhere inside you so it can be used where it is needed. And you have blood vessels everywhere in your entire body.

There is a lot in the food that is of no use to the body and this goes right through you and out of your body as faeces when you go to the lavatory. Water and other things are also carried out as urine.

When you were lying inside your mother, you could not eat with your mouth. You received nourishment through the blood so there were no faeces to get rid of. During the last few days you were in your mother's tummy, you drank the amniotic fluid and urinated into it too.

In your tummy, right in front, you have a hollow called the navel. Before you were born there was a tube there called the umbilical cord. The blood vessel running through this cord gave you all the nourishment you needed to live and grow. The other end of the cord joined the womb where the wall was especially thick. This thick part is called the placenta. In the placenta the blood vessels of the mother and the foetus lie very close and here nourishment and oxygen pass from

In the centre of this picture you can see the umbilical cord and the blood vessels inside it. The cord goes from the tummy of the foetus through the amnion into the placenta. There the big blood vessels separate into many small vessels that lie very close to the small blood vessels of the mother.

When you were born the midwife cut your cord but it healed quickly and what is left now is the navel, a small dent in your tummy.

This is what a foetus looks like when it is nine weeks old and 1½ inches [4 centimetres] long. The head and neck are equally thick. The arms and legs are still very short.

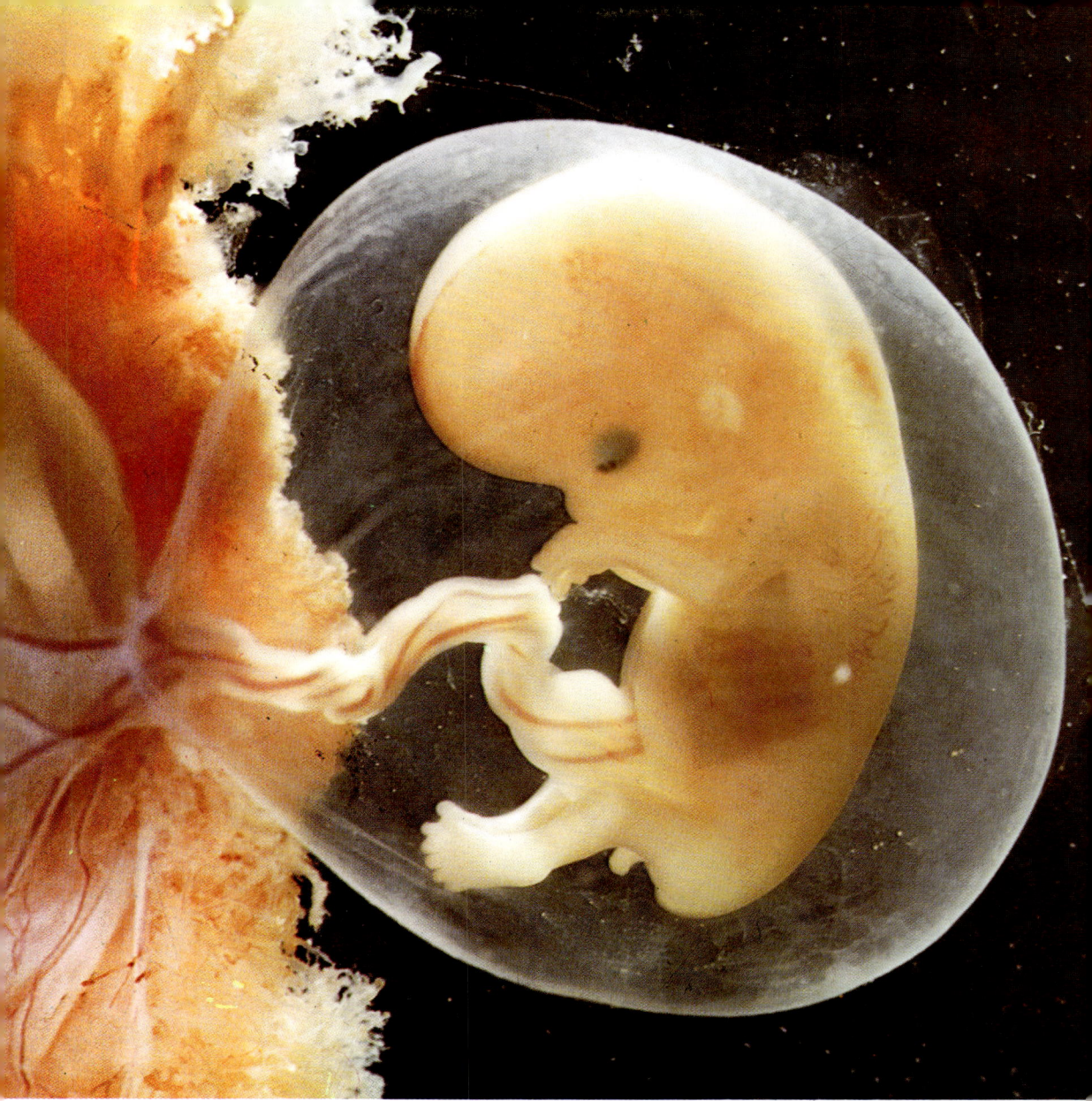

the blood of the mother to that of the foetus. In the same way the blood from the baby can also get rid of a lot of stuff which the baby does not need and cannot use any more. After it has gone into the mother's blood she gets rid of it when she goes to the lavatory or even when she breathes out.

The tail and other odd things

For a short time, before we were born, both you and I had a tail. When you had grown a little bit as a foetus and were about five weeks old you had a visible tail. In the big picture you can see what you looked like when you had been in the womb for about five weeks. The tail is curved: it is the pointed part that shows between the short, growing legs. But you were very small then. When you went on growing the tail disappeared.

The little human foetus looks like the little foetus of lots of other animals in almost every way. During the sixth week there were small slits on your neck. A fish foetus has also got these slits. When the fish grows, these slits become gills and the fish breathes with them down in the water and gets oxygen that way. There is oxygen in the water too, where the fish swims, not only in the air. But you grew out of the slits – you never needed them for breathing.

Humans and other animals are very much alike in many ways, as you know. We have eyes, nose, stomach and legs and so have lots of animals. To begin with, the different parts of the body of lots of animals start growing in just about the same way. But after a time each kind of animal develops in its own particular way, and we in ours.

In the picture on the right you can see a small, curved and pointed tail sticking up between the little legs, which look more like paddles than things to walk on.

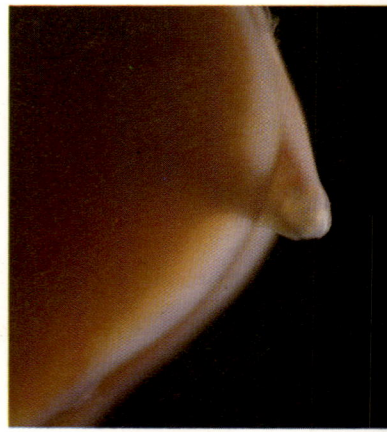

The tail is much smaller when the foetus is three months old.

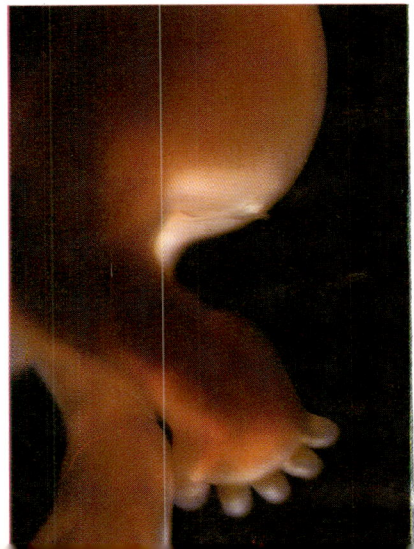

After about four months the tail has almost disappeared. There is just a tiny knob left and by the time the baby is born, that too has disappeared.

The third and fourth months

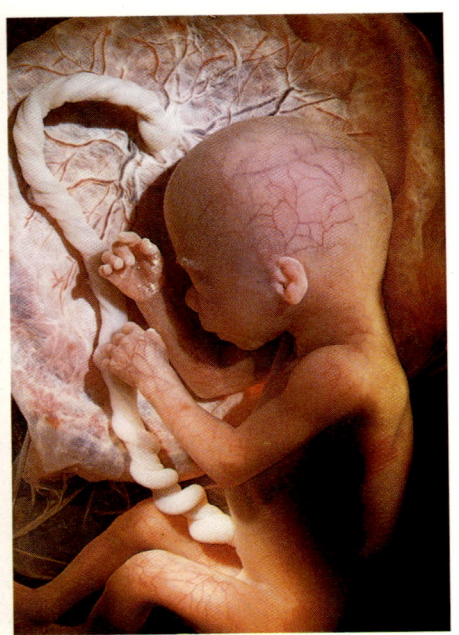

This is what you looked like after four months in there. You can see the cord clearly. The arms are longer than before and there is a proper neck. The ears are not quite completed yet. At this age you were about 6½ inches [16 centimetres] long and you weighed about 7 ounces [200 grammes].

During the first three months in the womb you could move about fairly freely without bumping against the walls. Your mother could feel you moving inside her – as if something was fluttering in there. You kicked with your legs and hammered with your fists and swung yourself around. A few months later when your mother's tummy was rather big you *did* hit the walls and your mother and father could watch as you kicked around inside. They could see your feet making your mother's tummy-wall bulge.

The more you grew inside her womb, the bigger your mother got. When you were five months old her tummy was very round. Anyone putting an ear close to her tummy could hear you moving around in there, and when the doctor checked up on your mother's health he also listened through his stethoscope and could hear your heart beating.

During the fourth month in the womb it was possible to see what you would look like when you were born. Your face was well organized with forehead, eyebrows, eyes, nose, mouth and so on. At this stage your eyes were closed while they grew. Your hands also nearly reached their final shape during this month. You lay in your amnion, just like the foetus shown here. The amnion cushions the foetus in a pool of fluid – so why doesn't it drown? Because it gets all the oxygen it wants through the cord from its mother, just as it gets its nourishment. This means it does not have to breathe. In fact it does not use its lungs at all until after it is born.

The last few months in the womb

At this stage you were growing in just about the same way as you and other children grow every day. You looked almost the same as when you were about to be born. Mostly you slept. But some of the time you were awake and kicked and made yourself felt. Sometimes a loud noise startled you because you could hear quite well in there.

Towards the end it was very cramped and you lay curled up tightly. Your hair began to grow all over your body. Some babies are born with soft hair on their ears and foreheads, but most lose their hair before they are born. All the time you were lying in the cushioning fluid, you were protected by a layer of grease over your body which stopped your skin going crinkly.

It finally grows cramped for the baby in the womb. It has to lie tightly curled up. But when you were as small as this, you were pliant and soft and none of the bones in your body were very long or very hard so it did not matter.

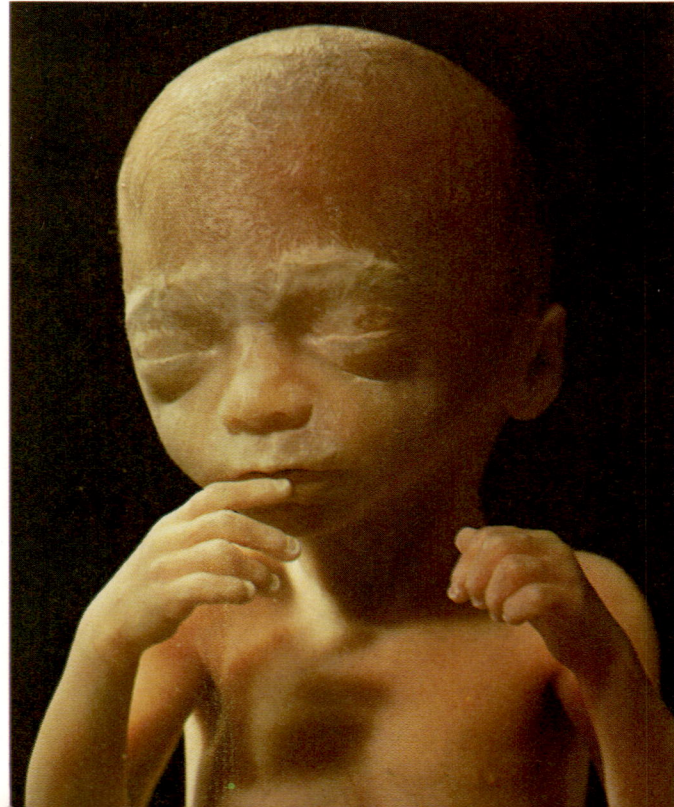

You were covered with grease when you lay in the amniotic fluid. You can see that very clearly in this picture – especially on the lips and eyebrows. This is what a foetus looks like when it is six months old.

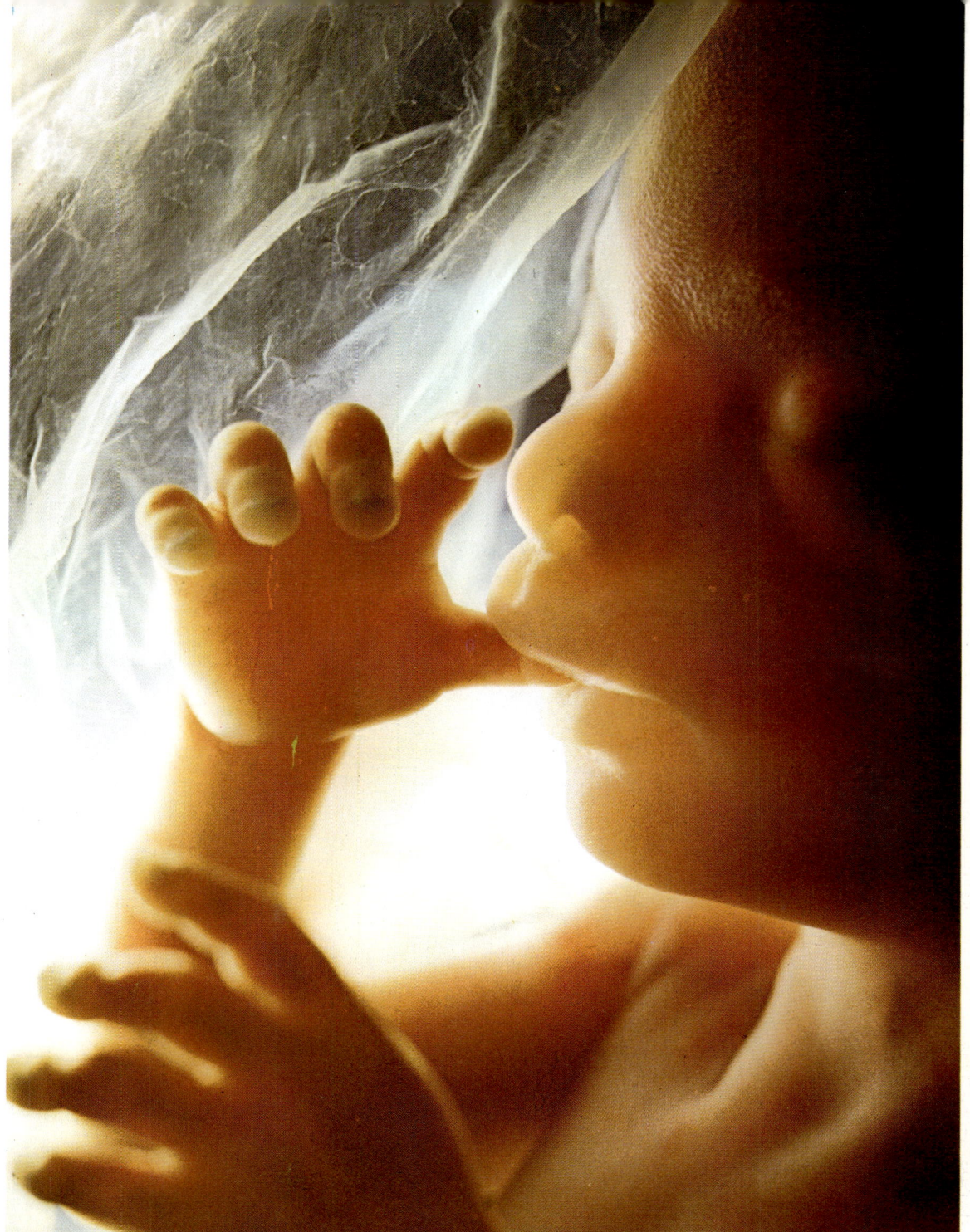

When you were four-and-a-half months old you began behaving like a new-born baby. Sometimes you had your thumb in your mouth. You did this not as a comfort, but as a kind of practice sucking, ready for when you wanted your mother's breast.

On your birth-day

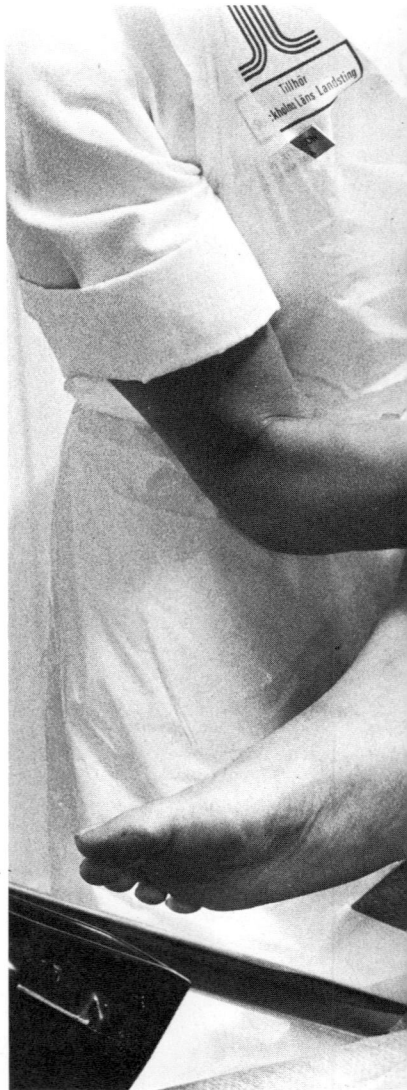

You came out of your mother's body through the slit she has between her legs. When your whole body was coming out through there, the slit was stretched out and was much wider than usual. This does not matter because women are very elastic and soft there. Afterwards the slit narrowed again. So that you could come out, the womb squeezed and let go, squeezed and let go, and you were pressed out. The squeezes are called contractions because the muscles of the womb get shorter when they are giving the baby a squeeze. Babies are usually born head first.

The womb has strong muscles in its walls and when they contract they press the baby downwards and out towards the slit. When this has been going on for some time the slit widens. The fluid runs out when the amnion bursts and the baby is pressed out. In the picture you can see how the baby is coming out and how the midwife, who helps the mother, holds the baby in her hands. Just after all the baby has come out, the placenta follows. Then the midwife sees to it that the baby has started breathing properly and finally she cuts the cord.

When you were born you were given a bath. Then you were weighed on the scales and measured. You did not need any food the first day. A day or two later you were given your mother's breast where you could suck the milk she had made there for you. Sometimes the mother has no milk in her breasts and then the baby has to have food from a bottle with a teat. When that happens father can feed the baby, too.

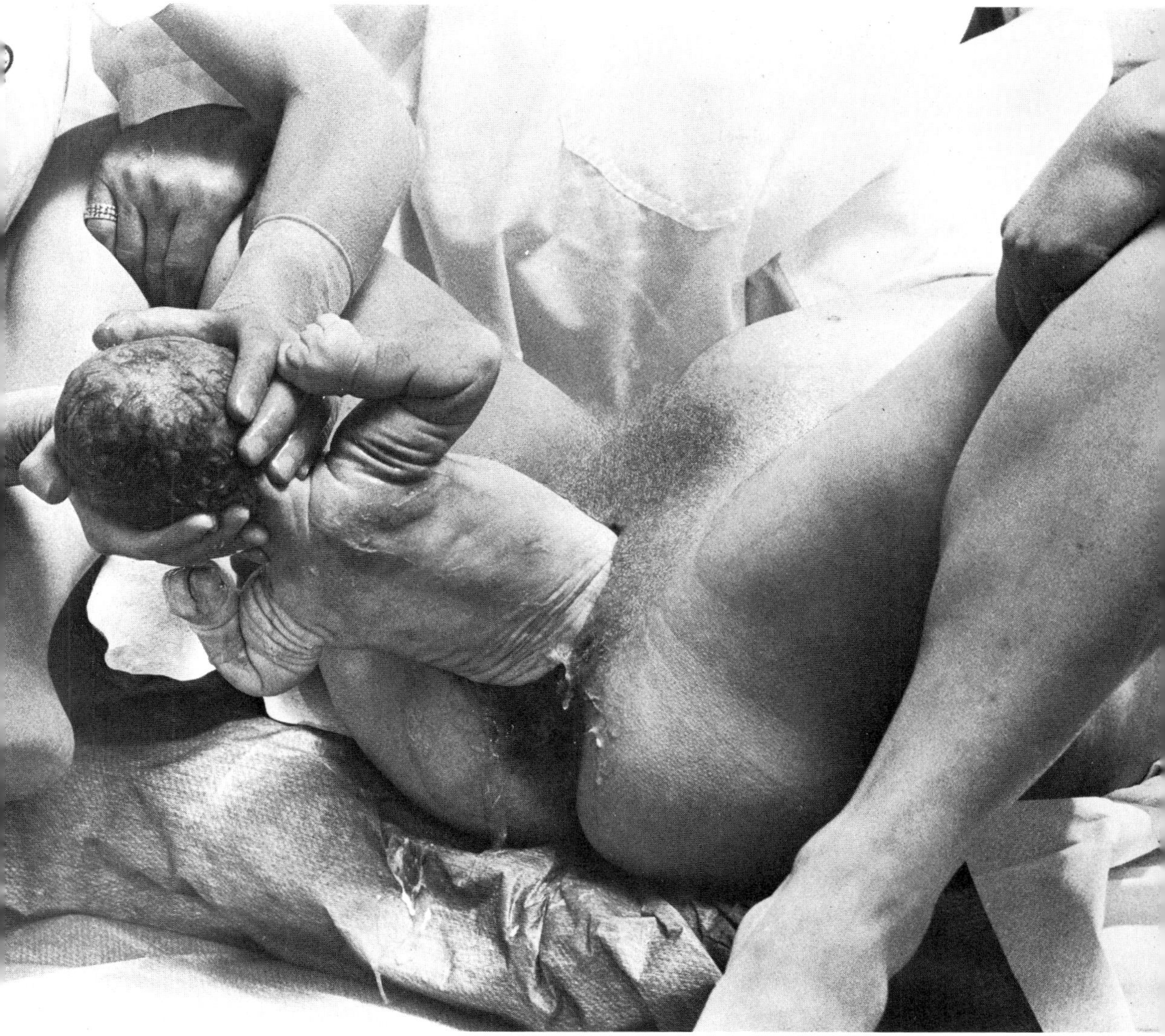

One minute after you were born you probably looked as tired as this baby because being born is hard work for the baby as well as the mother.

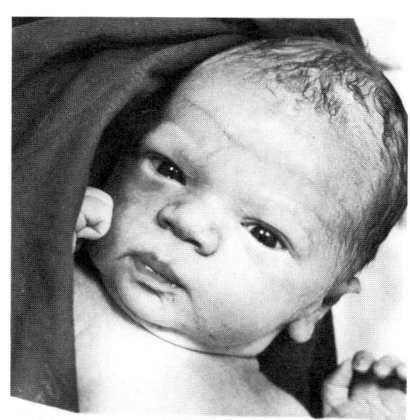

Here you can see three girls and a grown woman. The girls are 8, 14 and 4 years old. The woman is 24. The breasts – where babies can suck milk – begin to grow when girls are 10 to 14 years old and they begin to get hair on their pubis at about the same time.

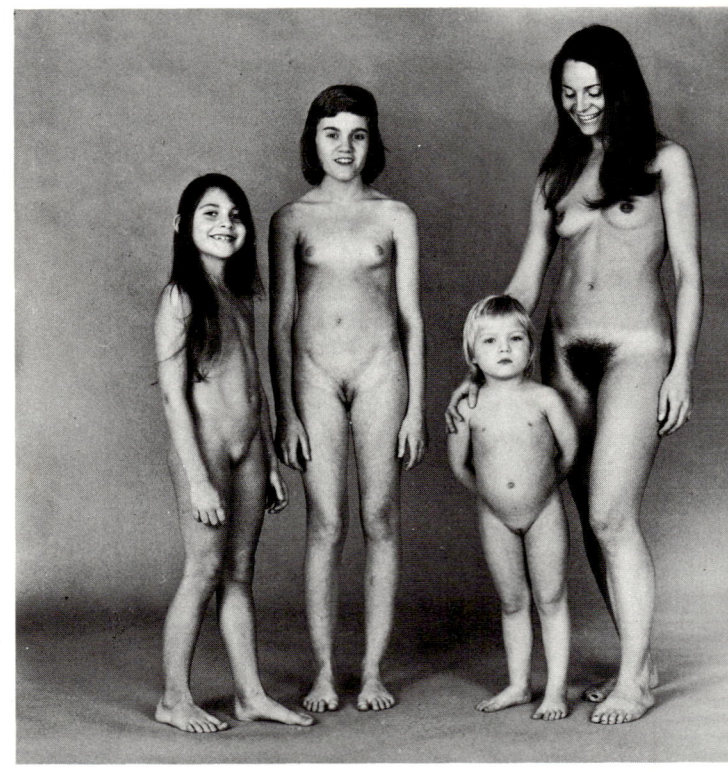

The body changes when you grow. In the beginning there is not much difference between boys and girls. The boy has a penis. When boys grow into men they become stronger and have bigger muscles. The man here is 23 years old, the boys are 4, 16 and 10. Most boys' penises are fully grown by the time they are 16 and most boys have deeper voices by then. Different boys have different size penises but that is not important. Boys grow hair around their penises and on their faces. The hair round the penis is fully grown by the time boys are 18, and their beards about two years later.

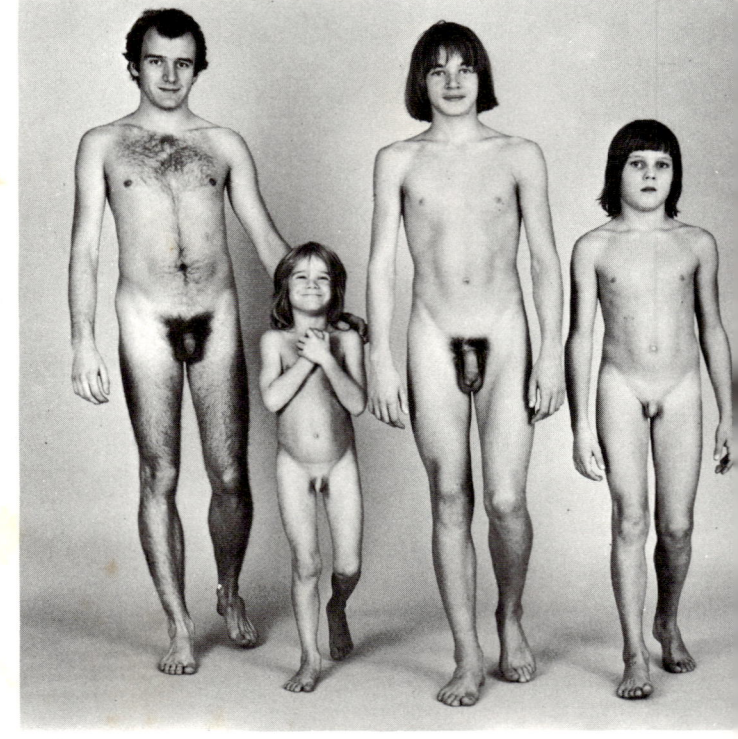

How did you get in?

So you came out of your mother on your birth-day. For nine months you had been in there, growing from one cell, as small as the point of a pin, into millions of cells – into a baby. But how did you get in there in the first place?

Just like everybody else you began by two small cells coming together and making one cell, a fertilized egg cell that could grow and divide itself. Your father produced a cell called the sperm cell and your mother produced the egg cell. Human cells are no bigger than the tiniest dot you can make with a pencil. The egg came from your mother's ovaries. She has two ovaries which are exactly alike. They are placed one on each side and a little above the womb, one on the right and one on the left.

A sperm cell can only be seen through a microscope. These sperm cells are produced in thousands in a grown man's testes, which are in a pouch of skin under his penis. The sperm cells are carried through a tube up into his body and then out through another tube, called the urethra, where his urine goes.

The green parts in this diagram show the position of a woman's genital organs. At the top are the ovaries. The Fallopian tubes begin next to them and end in the womb. The bottom of the womb opens into the vagina and the vagina ends in the slit which can be seen from the outside.

How are children made?

When a mother and a father want to start a baby they begin by lying beside each other, naked, and hugging and kissing. The father's penis becomes hard when they lie like this and he puts it into the opening between the mother's legs, the same opening where the baby will one day come out

The red parts show the position of a man's genital organs. The testes lie in the pouch below the penis. Here the tubes that carry the sperms begin, and they empty through the urethra.

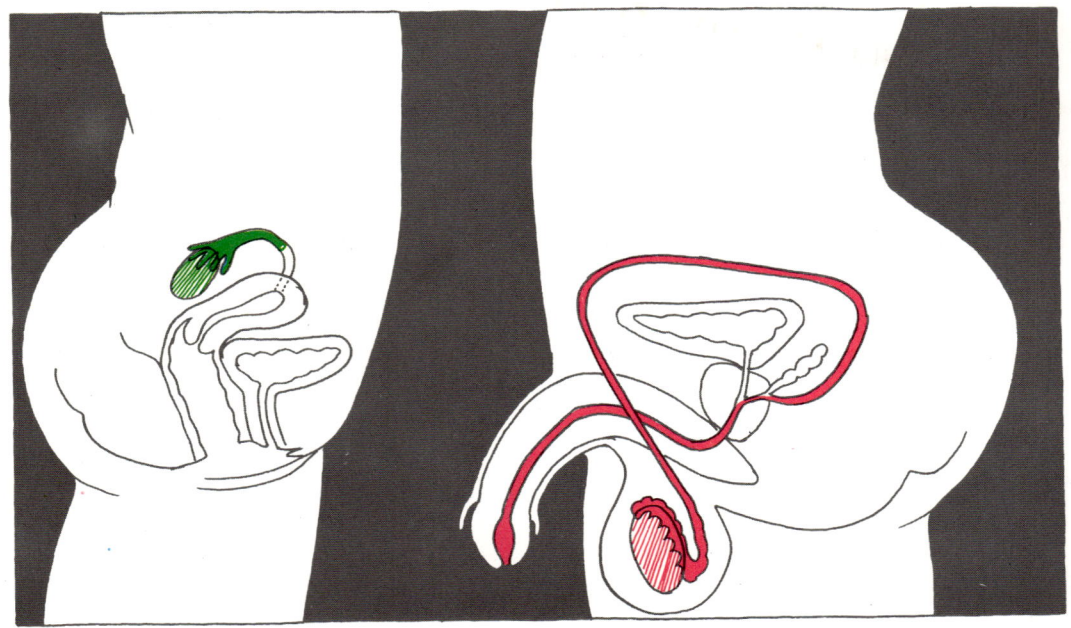

from. Then they move so that the penis slides into the tube that leads to the womb, the vagina. They feel lovely and loving while they are doing this and after a time the sperm cells jet out of the father's penis into the mother's vagina.

When the sperms are in the vagina they begin the long swim up into the womb, and then from the womb into the tubes, called the Fallopian tubes, which lead the eggs from the ovaries. In one of these tubes a sperm cell meets an egg cell and joins with it – when that happens a baby is started.

The penis is made so that it can stand up and become hard and go into the vagina easily. There are spaces inside it which can fill with blood, like your cheeks do when you blush, and so make it stand up, like a rubber glove does when you fill it with water. The penis can become hard without mother and father lying together, and they can enjoy the lovely and loving feeling of the penis sliding into the vagina without wanting to start a baby.

The egg cell in the Fallopian tube has come from one of the ovaries. In each of the two ovaries there are thousands of egg cells. Once a month one of the ovaries lets an egg cell go. In the tube the egg

These diagrams show the position of the genital organs.

On the left is a woman. Near the bottom of the diagram, by the leg, is the vagina. In front of it is the bladder and leading out from this the tube through which the urine passes. The vagina ends at the womb. At the top, coloured green in the diagram, is one of the ovaries and a Fallopian tube where the egg can be fertilized. The green colour shows the way the egg travels.

On the right is a man. His penis stands out. The urine is collected in his bladder and goes from there down through a tube and out through the penis. Behind the bladder there are two bags containing the fluid where the sperms can live. You can only see one of these bags in the picture. The sperms are formed in the testes which lie in the scrotum further down. The red colour shows the way the sperms travel from the scrotum through a tube which leads into the urine tube (or urethra), then through the penis and out of the body.

travels towards the womb. The egg cell travels very slowly. If it gets fertilized by a sperm cell, a baby begins as an embryo or foetus. This clings to the wall of the womb. And there it starts growing.

If the egg does not get fertilized on its journey from the ovary down the tube to the womb there will be no baby and the egg is carried out of the body. Very few eggs are fertilized. Those that are not are carried out of the body by menstruation, the monthly period. This appears like blood from the slit.

When a baby is made, a sperm cell meets an egg cell in the Fallopian tube. It is hard work for the tiny sperm cells to swim from the vagina through the womb and up the Fallopian tube. The sperm cell that gets there first meets the egg cell, and breaks through the wall of the egg. Then the two cells unite. They both become one new cell, the fertilized egg cell. This union is called conception. And it was during conception that you were made. Together your father and mother conceived a new human being – your mother became pregnant and you were on your way.

This cross-section drawing shows what it looks like when mother and father lie together. This is called sexual intercourse. The penis is inside the vagina. The red colour shows the long way the sperms have to travel from the testes to the ovaries. At the end of intercourse the sperm tubes and the sperm bags contract so the sperms are pressed out of the penis and into the vagina. There they start swimming under their own power through the womb and into the Fallopian tubes. Only one of the many sperms may fertilize an egg. The egg's way from an ovary to the Fallopian tube is marked in green. The fertilized egg is then carried into the womb where it develops into a baby.

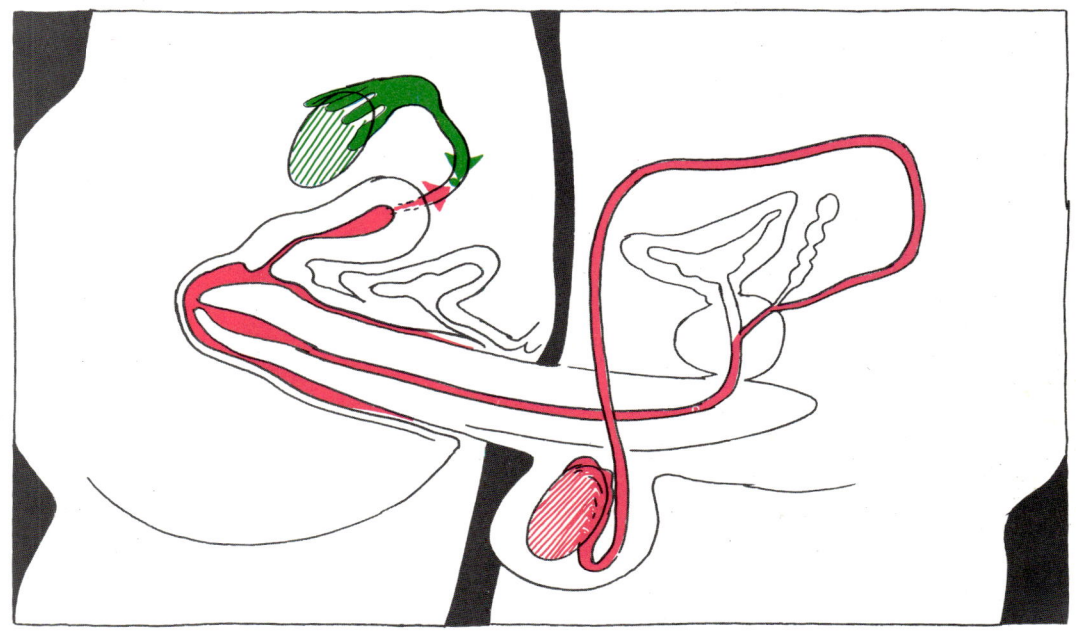

The sperms swim to the egg

The sperms swim hard towards the egg. The sperm is a cell with a head and a tail which it wiggles in order to swim through the fluid in which it lives. Both sperms and eggs live in this fluid. They cannot live in the air because then they will dry up. You can see the egg in the picture on the right. This egg is photographed in the Fallopian tube where it can be fertilized as it is slowly carried down towards the womb. The white dots around it are the sperms.

The egg on the right is on its way into the Fallopian tube where it can be fertilized. In reality it is not bigger than a very small dot. In the picture it is surrounded by sperms, which look like white dots.

Sperms on their way to the egg. This picture is very much enlarged so that the sperms can be seen. They cannot usually be seen with the naked eye.

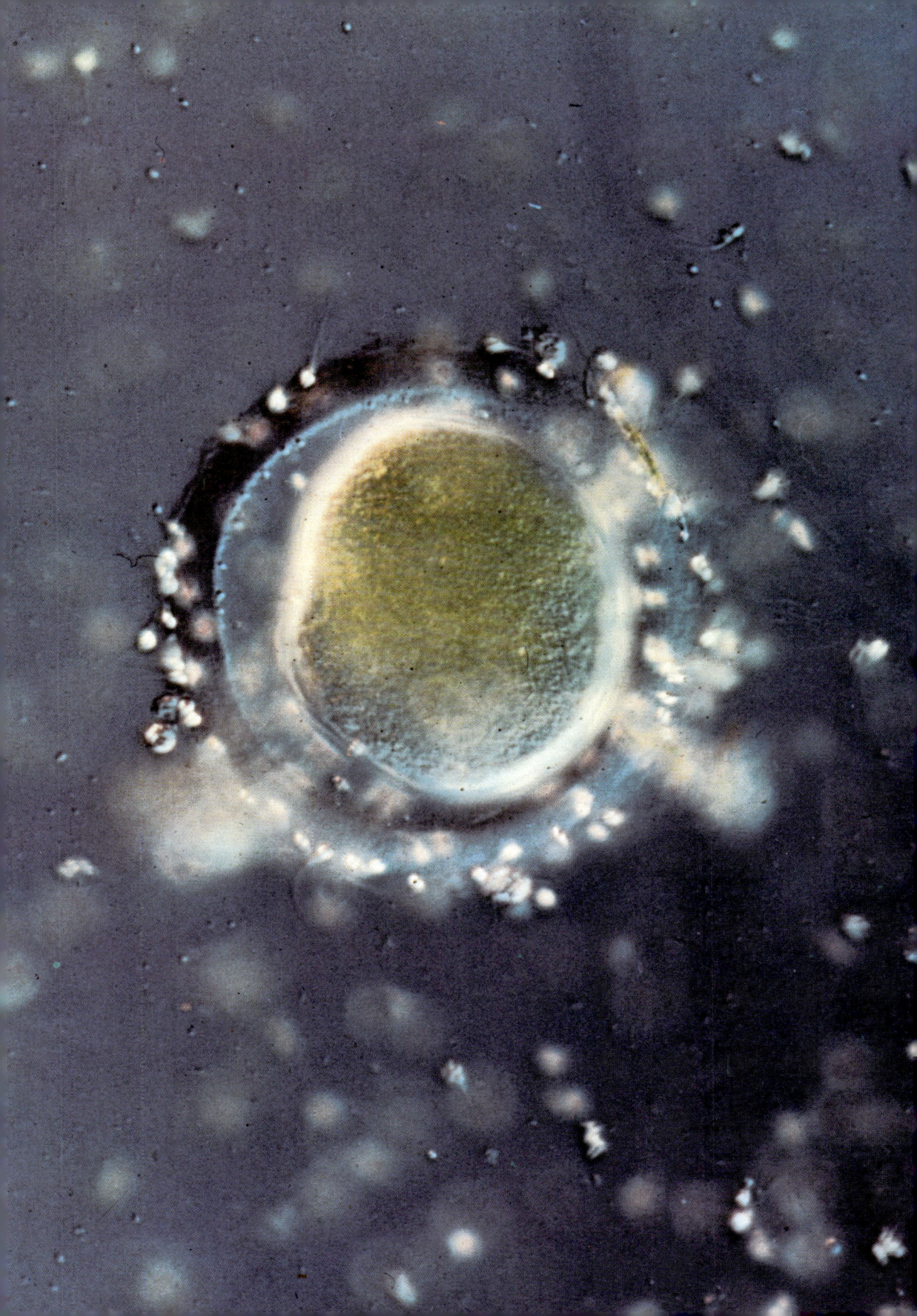

When you were conceived

On the left you can see some sperms which have finally reached the egg after their long journey. For such a small cell it really is a long way to travel. Two sperms have reached the egg almost at the same time. When one sperm has pushed its way into the egg, the egg is fertilized. As soon as one of them has forced its way through the wall of

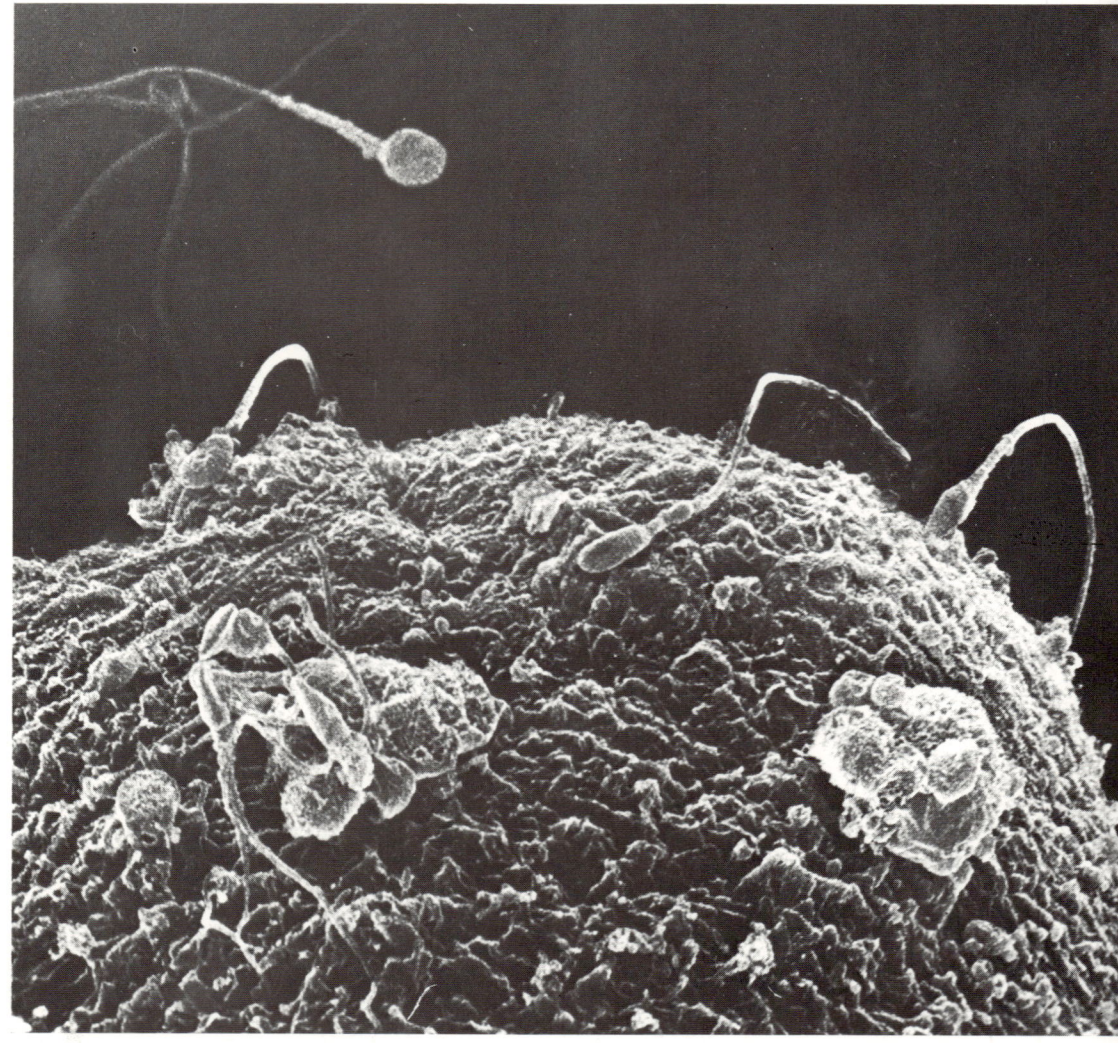

Some sperms are near the egg and one you can see above it. Only one single sperm out of all the thousands from the father joins with an egg and fertilizes it and so begins the marvellous growth of a human being.

the egg the wall becomes hard and will not let another sperm in.

On the right you can see how a sperm has reached the wall of one egg and is on its way in.

When the sperm has forced itself into the egg, the two join and become a new and bigger cell which is called a fertilized egg cell. This cell, in turn, starts dividing itself and that is how the baby starts growing. At the very moment the egg becomes fertilized you become you. A new human being emerges from the fertilized egg cell.

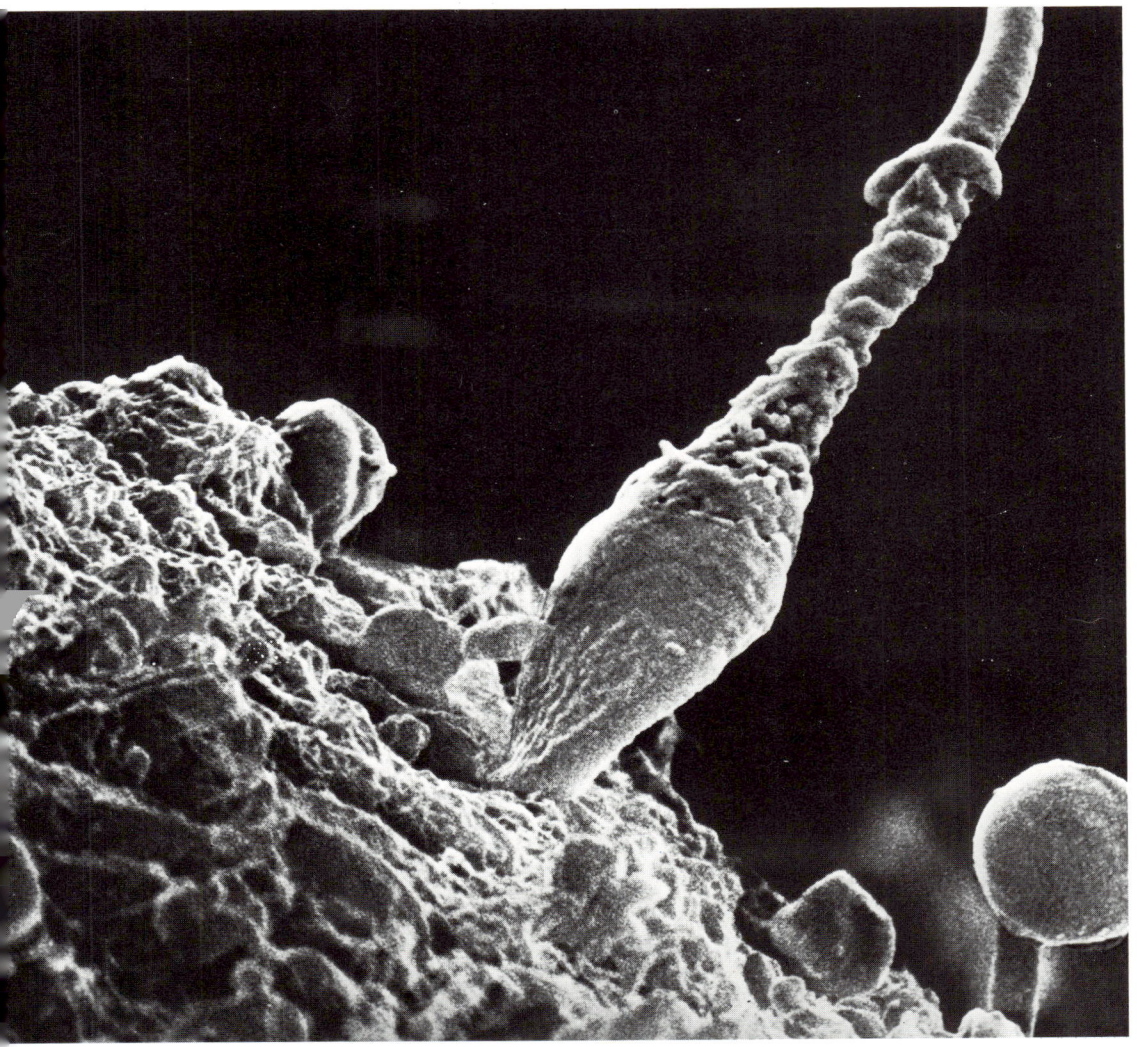

Here is a very much enlarged sperm.
It is just bumping against the wall of the egg
before pushing its way in to fertilize it.

27

In the beginning you were very small

A fertilized egg divides itself into two cells. These two cells each divide themselves into two and become four. The four become eight, the eight become sixteen and so on. More and more cells develop. The first division happens only a few hours after fertilization. At first the cells look like a lump. But they soon form themselves into something like a hollow ball. One side becomes dented as if the ball has been squeezed. Then the dented ball folds itself and becomes a tube and now the embryo is on its way to start looking like a baby.

In these photographs you can see the cells increasing. On the right is the tiny tube-shaped foetus after about four weeks. All those divisions and a lot of growth and energy have gone into its making.

The parts which one day will be the head and arms are beginning to stick out of the tube. And so the foetus goes on growing and growing as you already know and as you read about in the beginning of this book.

You can see here how the egg divides itself. One cell becomes two, then four.

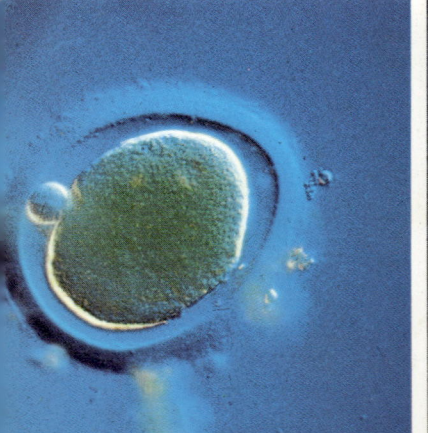
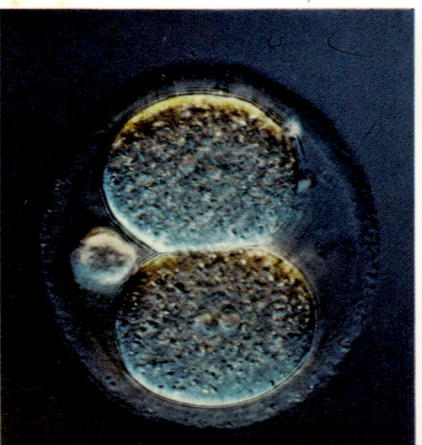

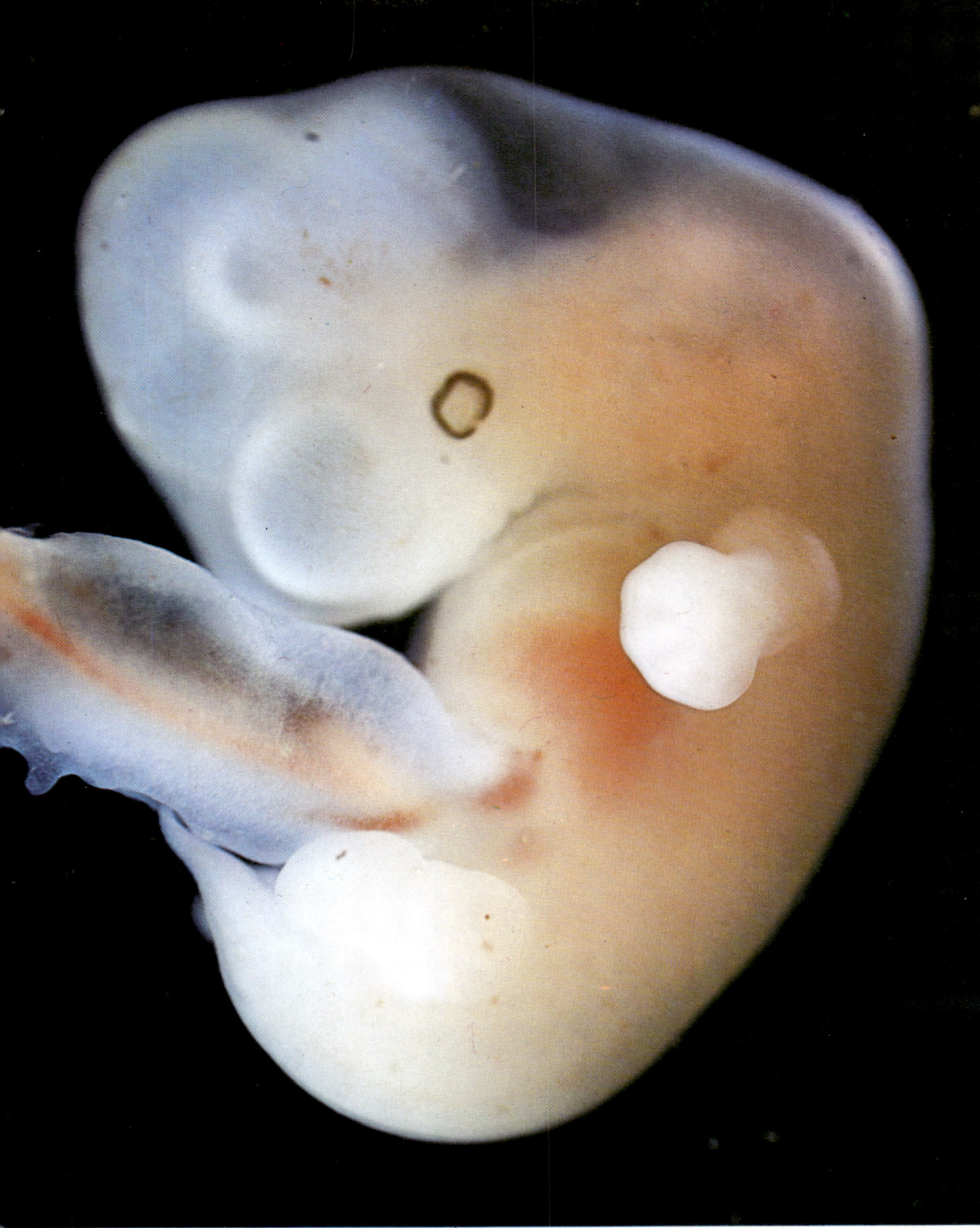

In this picture you can see what you looked like when you were four weeks old. The little circle above the middle in the picture is the beginning of an eye. To the right is the beginning of a hand. The foetus ends in a pointed tail. As you know, it disappears later. To the left you can see the cord.

When you came into the world

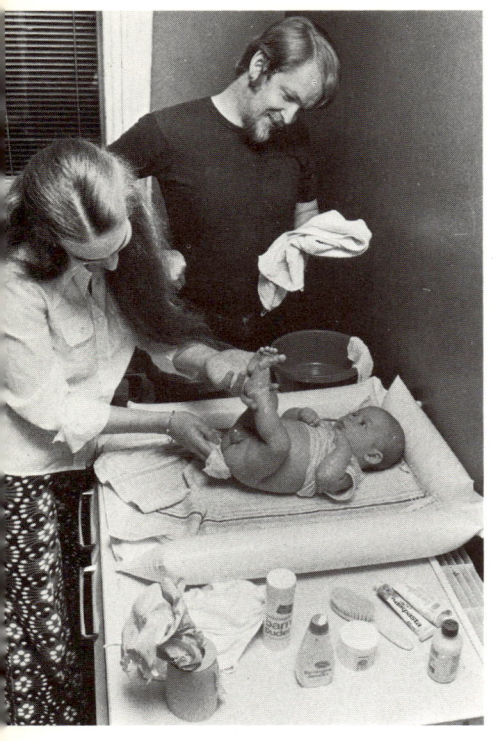

Your mother looked after you, or perhaps your aunt, or your gran, and your father helped too. New-born babies cannot look after themselves at all. Only the young of very simple animals like flies or frogs can do that. A kitten or calf has to have milk from its mother so that it can live.

You have probably heard someone say that you look like your mother or your father, or perhaps someone else in the family. Children often resemble other relatives, because many characteristics, also called genes, are inherited – among them is your appearance. The colour of the hair, for instance, is often inherited.

The development of all foetuses, from the fertilized egg right up to the baby, is directed by the characteristics given to the fertilized egg. Half of the genes come from the mother and half from the father. They, in turn, received their genes from their parents who got them from theirs and so on back in time. The genes are mixed as they always come from two parents at a time, and no human being in the world is quite like any other.

For many years you will need someone to take care of you and give you food or help. As you grow older you will gradually learn to look after yourself and when you finally become grown up, you will probably have children of your own to take care of.

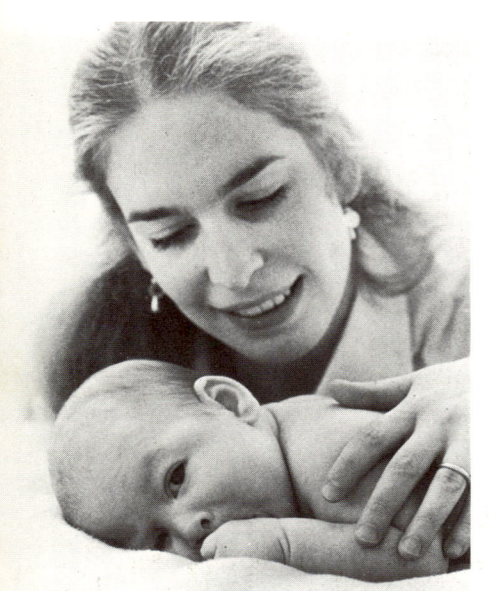

Mother and father help each other to tend their baby.